THE MAN

OF HE.

AND S/

THE MANAGEMENT
OF HEALTH
AND SAFETY

BY APAU

The Industrial Society

First published 1988 by
The Industrial Society
Robert Hyde House
48 Bryanston Square
London W1H 7LN
Telephone: 071–262 2401

Reprinted May 1990

© *The Industrial Society, 1988*

ISBN 0 85290 409 6

Printed by Lithosphere
☎ 071–700 6545

CONTENTS

FOREWORD

Efficient management of occupational health and safety is increasingly recognised by modern management as an essential ingredient of commercial success. This Notes for Managers has been written by Inspectors in the Health and Safety Executive's Accident Prevention Advisory Unit (APAU) and has its origins in their practical experience in the wide range of industrial, commercial and public undertakings which have been examined by the Unit. It is not only essential reading for all managers but is also useful to those arranging courses for senior staff to alert decision-makers in companies to the potential benefits that a properly managed health and safety policy can provide.

APAU is a small team within the Health and Safety Executive Headquarters organisation. Its staff have wide experience of auditing the health and safety performance of companies and public undertakings nationwide. The Unit has developed computer databases for accident analysis on behalf of HSE and produced numerous publications on occupational health and safety.

F. D. LINDSAY
Director, APAU

1 WHY MANAGE HEALTH AND SAFETY?

Health and safety, like other aspects of an organisation's activities, such as production, cost control or quality assurance, need to be effectively managed if the aims and objectives of the organisation are to be realised.

The minimum aims and objectives in relation to health and safety should be to ensure, so far as is reasonably practicable, that employees and members of the public are not exposed to unacceptable risk as a result of the organisation's activities. These objectives are legal obligations under the Health and Safety at Work Act 1974.

THE CRUCIAL ROLE OF MANAGERS

Although most health and safety legislation places the duty of compliance firmly on the body corporate (ie the company), this duty can only be discharged by the effective action of its managers. Time and again studies by the Accident Prevention Advisory Unit have shown that the vast majority of fatal accidents and those causing serious injury could have been prevented by management action.

1. During the period 1981–1985, 739 people were killed in the construction industry. Ninety per cent of these deaths could have been prevented. In 70 per cent of cases positive action by management could have saved lives.[1]

2. A study of 326 fatal accidents during maintenance activities occurring between 1980 and 1982 inclusive showed that in 70 per cent of the cases positive management actions could have saved lives.[2]

3. A study of maintenance accidents in the chemical industry between 1982 and 1985 demonstrated that 75 per cent

were the result of management failing to take reasonably practicable precautions.[3]

Since 1981, although the total number of fatal injuries at work has remained more or less constant, there has been a substantial rise in reported major injuries which must give cause for concern. Combined fatal and major injury incidence rates have risen by some 31 per cent in manufacturing, 34 per cent in agriculture and 45 per cent in construction[4] and at the time of writing there is no sign that this trend has been arrested. Every year around 500 people are killed and some 400,000 accidents at work causing more than three days absence are reported to enforcing authorities. Available evidence suggests that many non-fatal accidents still go unreported.

It should not be forgotten that more people die from occupational diseases than from accidents at work.

ACCIDENTS AND OCCUPATIONAL ILL HEALTH COST MORE THAN MONEY

Every accident and case of occupational ill health involves not only a cost to the individual, family and friends in terms of pain and suffering but also financial costs borne by the individual, the employer and the exchequer. It is difficult to be precise about the costs of accidents as there is no agreed basis for calculating them, but a study in 1981[5] estimated that the resource costs in 1978/79 of occupational accidents were between £700m and £1,400m (recalculation at 1987 prices puts this figure at £1370m–£2740m) and that of prescribed industrial diseases diagnosed in 1978/79 at £56m (£109m at 1987 prices).

DuPont[6] have recently reported that a disabling injury in the chemical industry (involving loss of at lease one shift) costs $18,650. In the USA, an average chemical company with 1000 employees could expect to have nine lost workday injuries and, given the estimated profit margin of 3.75 per cent, would need $4.5m in sales to offset these injuries.

Although the total cost of personal-injury accidents may be difficult to establish, some estimated costs in terms of damage to plant and equipment and production losses resulting from large-scale incidents have been published. For example, at Flixborough in 1974, the direct damage to the plant was estimated at £20.5m or £77m total reconstruction cost of plant and surrounding property (£77m and £290m in 1987).[7] In addition to the dreadful human toll, the direct and indirect financial consequences of the Piper Alpha disaster are likely to dwarf these figures.

There is no doubt that occupational accidents and ill health do impose substantial costs on industry, and costs are of vital importance to managers. Management of health and safety can therefore be considered as essential to an overall loss control programme.

There are other reasons why firms need to manage health and safety. The public is now increasingly aware of the interface between industry and the environment and industrialists need to acknowledge this concern. Failure to manage health and safety can have important commercial implications. An international company has so far been unable to obtain planning permission for a new plant in a particular part of the United Kingdom following a major incident in one of their chemical plants abroad. This was despite the fact that the chemicals involved in the proposed new plant bore no relation to those present in the plant where the incident occurred.

In the United Kingdom, the law requires health and safety to be managed to ensure, so far as is reasonably practicable, that employees (and non employees) are not exposed to risks to their health and safety. A major company was recently fined £750,000 for failing to comply with their duties under the Health and Safety at Work Act 1974. Other costs associated with the incident ran into many millions of pounds. Small firms are often particularly vulnerable to the costs of accidents and work-related ill health. The loss of a single key worker is often more acutely felt in a small firm than in a large one; it may be harder to replace damaged plant, and the resultant higher insurance premiums may make all the difference between profit and loss.

In addition to the legal obligations on the company, individual managers have legal obligations both in terms of their positions as employees and also in their specific roles as directors, managers, secretaries or officers of the company. Failure to comply with these obligations is an offence, and indeed some managers and directors have been prosecuted under the Health and Safety at Work Act. Similarly, in incidents where the safety of the general public is affected, the actions of managers and directors and perceived failure to manage health and safety are likely to be open to public scrutiny. The public inquiries into the disasters at Zeebrugge and King's Cross are but the latest examples.

THE BENEFITS OF MANAGING HEALTH AND SAFETY

Conversely, there are real benefits to be accrued from managing health and safety. There is ample evidence[8,9] that companies which have made a conscious decision to manage health and safety have reaped positive rewards as a result of their efforts in terms of reductions in accidents and ill health, consequential claims reductions, improved compliance with the law and better working conditions. Improved standards of health and safety have spin-offs in terms of better employee relationships, lower absenteeism and increased efficiency, better public image and bottom-line profitability. It is no accident that the firms with the best safety records in the UK are often numbered amongst the most profitable.

2 WHERE TO START

THE SAFETY POLICY

Section 2(3) of the Health and Safety at Work Act 1974 requires every employer (except where there are less than five employees) to prepare and, as often as may be appropriate, revise a written statement of the general policy with respect to the health and safety at work of employees and the organisation, and arrangements for carrying out that policy and to bring the statement and any revision of it to the notice of all his employees.

This written statement is generally referred to as the 'safety policy' and has a vital role to play in managing health and safety. It should be the reference document for the management of health and safety within the organisation. Advice is available on writing safety policies.[10] The basic elements are:

1. specifying objectives
2. organising to achieve the objectives
3. specifying the arrangements for carrying out the policy
4. monitoring of the effectiveness of the organisation and arrangements and the results they achieve, and revising policy accordingly.

SECURING COMMITMENT AND COMMUNICATION

Success in managing health and safety can only be achieved by having a clear corporate commitment. This commitment should not be merely words in a written document but should permeate the organisation; it is sometimes termed 'the safety culture'.

The lead must be given by the most senior executives within the company who must demonstrate that their commitment to health and safety is translated into positive action at successive levels throughout the organisation. They must ensure that health and safety has a high profile and take a personal interest in it. Without this leadership success is unlikely to be achieved. The Sheen Report[11] on the *Herald of Free Enterprise* capsize gave a useful exposition of the nature of duties and action expected of directors in dealing with health and safety. This theme has been continued in the Fennell Report[12] on the King's Cross Underground fire.

Once a clear lead has been established by senior managers, then middle and junior managers must also play their part. The company's rules and standards for health and safety must be observed by all staff. Subordinates soon perceive what managers regard as important and act accordingly. Managers must consistently illustrate by example that they give health and safety a high priority and not forget that, often, what a manager does not do or say is equally as important as what he does do or say. For example, a manager who walks past unguarded dangerous machinery without commenting, who fails to take action when he sees employees not wearing appropriate protective equipment or fails to take part in fire drills is implicitly accepting sub-standard conditions. This is readily perceived by the workforce who will carry on working dangerously, particularly if it makes life easier for them. Should an accident or incident occur, the manager can not then claim that the fault lay with the employees merely because they did not follow instructions.

Effective communication throughout the organisation plays a vital part in promoting the 'safety culture'. The safety representative and safety committee system should be effectively utilised as part of the communication process.

3 GETTING ORGANISED

WHO DOES WHAT?

Seeking to achieve objectives in health and safety is no different to achieving production or sales targets – it requires proper
organisation. Most successful organisations demonstrate the
following features:

- Unbroken and logical delegation of duties through line
  management to the supervisors who operate where the
  hazards arise and most accidents happen.
- Identification of key personnel, accountable to top management, who ensure that detailed arrangements for safe
  working are drawn up, implemented and maintained.
- Definition of the roles of line and functional management.
  Job descriptions should identify specific roles to avoid
  expensive and potentially dangerous overlapping. A
  concern for safety and health should be seen as an
  essential part of good management. Job descriptions
  should include health and safety and be agreed with the
  holder of a particular job, to ensure that he understands
  what he has to do. It is equally important that they define
  the limits of a particular role. For example, responsibility
  for taking direct action will normally lie with line
  management rather than with the safety officer or adviser.
  The safety adviser's role will probably include monitoring
  the effectiveness of safety procedures and the provision
  of information for senior management.
- Arrangements for adequate support by relevant functional management, not only by the safety adviser,
  but also, according to need, by the works doctor or
  nurse, the works engineers, designers, chemists, and
  so on. Where processes involve complex, technical
  hazards or particular occupational health considerations,
  an appropriate level of specialist advice is essential.

Sometimes it may be necessary to buy this in from consultants.

- Nomination of persons with the authority and competence to monitor safety performance both individually and collectively, by unit, by site or by department.
- Provision of the means to deal with failures to meet the requirements of the job as it has been described and agreed. Once a manager knows what he has to do and the means have been established for measuring what he has done, he must be held accountable for his management of safety and health in the same way as he would be for any other function. The organisation must indicate unambiguously to the individual exactly what he must do to fulfil his role; thereafter a failure is a failure to manage effectively.
- Making it known in terms of both time and money what resources are available for safety and health. The individual must be certain of the extent to which he is realistically supported by the policy and by the organisation needed to fulfil it.

ASSESSING THE RISKS

The nature of the hazards in the workplace must be identified and the related risks assessed. A good starting point is to identify the legislation applicable to the particular process or operation and then assess compliance with it. Published guidance on the legislation and on recognised standards may be consulted. The Health and Safety Executive produces a variety of publications[13], as do the British Standards Institute, some trade associations, and safety organisations.

Sections 2, 3, 4 and 6 of the Health and Safety at Work Act 1974 can also form a useful basis for making an assessment by listing topics (e.g. systems of work, supervision, training, safe place of work, working environment, etc.) which need to be addressed.

Health risks should also be assessed to establish the adequacy of existing occupational health provisions and to identify unmet needs for expert advice. The assessment should include the prevention of occupational ill health, health aspects of job placement and rehabilitation, arrangements for first aid and treatment services and the use of the workplace as a focus for health-promotion activities.

The Health and Safety Executive has published advice on reviewing occupational health needs[14] and on essentials of health and safety at work, aimed at the smaller firm[15] which may be of particular assistance to managers.

SETTING CONTROL STANDARDS

Having established the nature and extent of the hazards and assessed the risks, they should be eliminated where possible. Where they cannot be eliminated, measures need to be taken to control them. The minimum control measures can be identified by reference to the legislation and recognised standards mentioned previously. The existing control measures can then be compared with the required standard and upgraded as necessary or, where they do not exist, be introduced. The control measures adopted should then be formalised into standards and procedures to enable them to be monitored. These should also cover the aspects of occupational health provision mentioned above.

Standards should be agreed in consultation with the people directly involved. A realistic approach taking account of how people actually work is required. Groups of employees often devise methods of working which are very different from those which managers believe they use. Sometimes these do not have any health and safety implications, but often they will. Where such implications are established then particular effort, mainly in time and persuasion, will be needed to convince people that a change is needed if they and their fellow workers are to be safeguarded.

Procedures must be clear, unambiguous and capable of being understood by the recipients. It is essential that they are relevant and kept up-to-date. All too often procedures do not keep pace with changes on the workshop floor and become irrelevant. Non-routine operations such as maintenance work also need to be included. Serious and fatal accidents are often associated with maintenance activities.

Although there is a general need to ensure that procedures and standards are written and adopted, it is important to ensure that both managers and employers are not overwhelmed with paperwork, as this may produce an adverse reaction.

A useful approach is to have a safety/procedure manual as a source of reference, with checklists and edited procedures for use as working documents.

4 MONITORING FOR EFFECT

Managers are accustomed to evaluating performance against targets in their everyday work, and measurement by whatever means is an essential element in achieving stated objectives. Health and safety are no different.

The primary aim of measurement is to ensure that the standards achieved at the workplace conform as closely as possible to the objectives of the organisation. The secondary aim is to provide information to justify either a change of course or a revision of the original goals. By comparing the actual results with those originally hoped for, corrective action may be taken as necessary.

ACCIDENT INCIDENCE RATES

How is health and safety performance measured? Perhaps a manager's first reaction is to look at the accident statistics for his own department or company, either in terms of total number of accidents, or incidence and frequency rates:

the accident incidence rate =

$$\frac{total\ number\ of\ reported\ accidents}{total\ number\ of\ employees} \times 1000$$

and

the accident frequency rate =

$$\frac{total\ number\ of\ accidents\ (time\ lost > one\ shift\ or\ day)}{total\ number\ of\ man\ hours\ worked} \times 100,000$$

These can then be compared over time or with the performance of others engaged in similar activities. The Health and Safety Executive publishes incidence rates for the major industrial classifications. Although accident rates are one indicator they do not tell the whole story. The unreliability of historical accident data as a guide to future performance has been recognised for years. Accident reporting criteria can be subject to influences which have nothing to do with safety performance, e.g. different individuals react differently to injuries of a similar nature, and there are geographical variations. There is no clear correlation between such measurements and work conditions, the injury potential or the severity of injuries which have occurred. Managers need to be aware of these limitations when looking at their own accident statistics and not be lulled into a misplaced sense of security merely because no accidents have been reported recently.

SAFETY AUDITS

What is a realistic measurement of safety performance? Measuring means making a comparison with a standard. In health and safety terms this means making assessments of compliance with standards and procedures introduced to maintain health and safety performance with agreed objectives. Hence the importance of having standards and procedures which are clearly defined and written down, making them amenable to audit. Audits can help to assess the standard of managerial control by identifying sub-standard conditions and initiating remedial action; the achievement of good standards by managers and staff can be recognised and performance evaluated over a period.

Some companies have devised their own audit schemes involving scoring systems whereby points are awarded under various topic headings. Other companies prefer more qualitative audit systems. There is no hard and fast rule except that monitoring is necessary. What gets measured gets done. A number of proprietary health and safety monitoring schemes are now available in the UK. The benefits of any scheme, be it proprietary or in-house, are dependent upon the level of commitment by senior management and all those involved in its implementation. It is for each undertaking to determine which scheme is best suited to its needs and, in the case of proprietary systems, this involves making choices on costs and potential benefits.

5 ACCIDENT/INCIDENT INVESTIGATION

WHY INVESTIGATE?

Although the majority of companies investigate accidents which involve serious injury, managers should be alert to the possibility that the difference between a serious or even a fatal injury accident and a non-injury incident can sometimes be measured in terms of inches or seconds. Relatively minor incidents may therefore require thorough investigation based on their potential to have caused injury or plant loss. The severity of the injury therefore should not be the only criterion for a thorough investigation. Accident investigation helps to identify weaknesses in safety systems or in the way they are being applied.

Managers should be aware of the concept of accident triangles which describe the approximate relationship between the numbers of fatal and major-injury accidents, lost-time accidents, property-damage incidents and near misses. The following ratios have been reported.[16]

For every one serious injury accident:

- there were 10 minor injury accidents;
- there were 30 incidents involving property damage;
- there were 600 near misses.

HUMAN FACTORS

Company accident-report forms often include sections to describe the circumstances of the accident and for managers' comments. Examination of such reports often reveals phrases such as 'did not comply with instructions', 'was not paying attention' or 'injured person was careless'. Managers' comments often take the form of 'told to take more care', 'more training required' and 'guard repaired'.

There is sometimes a tendency to consider that if an accident occurs then it is more likely that the injured person was the agent of his own misfortune and only had himself to blame, or that the accident was the result of 'human error'. All too often ascribing an accident to human error is seen as sufficient explanation in itself, precluding further attempts to look for the underlying causes of that error.

It should be recognised that people do not make errors merely because they are careless or inattentive. Usually they have understandable (albeit incorrect) reasons for acting in the way they did. Most accidents have multiple causes and it is important that managers recognise this fact and look beyond the immediate cause of the injury. Invariably they will find that the incident itself was the culmination of a number of failures in management control and that the action/inaction of the individual(s) immediately involved was only the last link in the chain, and that the 'human error' cause was foreseeable and therefore amenable to control. The investigation of accidents and incidents should therefore look beyond the immediate cause of the injury to the fundamental causes. By analysing the incidents in this way and categorising causes, useful information and trends can be obtained. This enables resources to be targeted effectively.

6   TRAINING

Training is an essential ingredient of any successful safety policy and the lack of training is a major contributory cause in many accidents. It is perhaps the main source of human error.

SENIOR STAFF

It is particularly important to ensure that the key personnel who have special health and safety responsibilities within the organisation are properly trained. In the experience of APAU, health and safety training for managers, particularly those in senior positions, is often neglected; they are often the last people to recognise or admit to the need.

SUPERVISORS

Similarly, supervisors have a vital role to play in ensuring health and safety yet often they receive little or no specific training. Particular regard needs to be given to the need to train them in hazard identification in order that action can be taken to remove hazards from their area of control. Safety training should be an integral part of job training and of job specification.

NEW STARTERS

New starters to any job are particularly vulnerable and likely to have accidents. All new starters need to be trained in the essentials of health and safety relevant to their work before being put in a position where they are at risk or can become a hazard to others.

7   CHECKLIST FOR MANAGERS

The following questions are intended as an aid to managers. They are not exhaustive but are intended to cover the main issues addressed in the text.

WHERE TO START

- Do we have a safety policy statement? When was it last revised?

- Is it comprehensive? Does it specify the organisation (i.e. people and their responsibilities) and arrangements (i.e. systems and procedures)?

- How is the policy commitment to health and safety promoted throughout the organisation?

- How do individual managers demonstrate their own commitment?

- How is a 'safety culture' promoted?

ORGANISATION FOR HEALTH AND SAFETY

- Is the delegation of duties logical and successive throughout the organisation?

- How are people made aware of their responsibilities?

- Is final responsibility accepted by the relevant director?

- Are the health and safety responsibilities of senior managers specified in job descriptions?

- How is the safety performance of managers measured? Is it an ingredient of their annual review?

- Are the roles of key functional managers clearly defined?

- How are managers made aware of the requirements of health and safety legislation relative to their own departments?

- How is compliance with legal requirements assessed?

- Has a competent assessment been made of all hazards associated with the company's activities?

- Has an assessment been made of occupational health needs?

MONITORING FOR EFFECT

- Is there a comprehensive established system for monitoring compliance with standards and procedures?

- Are there sufficient staff with adequate knowledge and facilities to carry out the monitoring?

- How well do we comply with the law on health and safety?

- How far have we met our own policy objectives?

- What is our own accidents and ill health record? Is it acceptable?

- What deficiencies have we identified? How are they to be remedied? What more needs to be done? Now? Within the next year?

- Are the results of monitoring made available both to the managers concerned and to senior managers?

ACCIDENT/INCIDENT INVESTIGATION

- Are there clear criteria for reporting and investigating accidents and incidents?

- How well are they understood?

- How are near-miss incidents identified?

- How far does the accident-investigation system seek to identify fundamental causes and failure in management control?

- Is information obtained from accident investigation analysed to establish trends? Do we make good use of it?

TRAINING FOR HEALTH AND SAFETY

- What is the system for identifying training needs?

- Does health-and-safety training cover all levels from senior management to new entrant?

- What 'special risk' situations requiring training exist?

- Are sufficient people trained to cope?

NOTES

1 *Blackspot Construction: A Study of Five Years Fatal Accidents in the Building and Civil Engineering Industries.* HMSO 1988. ISBN 0 1188 3992 6.

2 *Deadly Maintenance: A Study of Fatal Accidents at Work.* HMSO 1985. ISBN 0 11883 806 7.

3 *Dangerous Maintenance: A study of Fatal Accidents in the Chemical Industry and How to Prevent Them.* HMSO 1987. ISBN 0 11883 957 8.

4 *Health and Safety Commission Report 1985-86.* ISBN 0 11883 925 X.

5 Costs of Occupational Accidents and Diseases in GB. P Morgan and N Davies. *Employment Gazette,* P477. November 1981.

6 *AM Paint Coatings* J., 20 April 1987, 16.

7 One Hundred Large Losses – A Thirty Year Review of Property Damage in the Hydrocarbon-Chemical Industries. Fred a Manuele. *Loss Prevention Bulletin* No. 058. August 1984.

8 *Success and Failure in Accident Prevention.* HMSO 1976. ISBN 0 11880 330 1.

9 *Managing Safety: A Review of the Role of Management in Occupational Health and Safety by the Accident Prevention Advisory Unit of HM Factory Inspectorate.* HMSO 1981. ISBN 0 11883 443 6.

10 *Effective Policies for Health and Safety.* HMSO (3rd impression) 1986. ISBN 0 11883 254 9.

11 *Herald of Free Enterprise* Report of Court No. 8074. Formal Investigation, paragraph 14. HMSO 1987. ISBN 0 11550 828 7.

12 Investigation into the King's Cross Underground fire. HMSO 1988. ISBN 0 101049 927.

13 Health and Safety Executive Library and Information Services Publications in Series: List July 1988.

14 *Review Your Occupational Health Needs: Employer's Guide*. HMSO 1988. ISBN 0 11883 993 4.

15 *Essentials of Health and Safety at Work*. HMSO 1988. ISBN 0 11883 977 2.

16 *Practical Loss Control Leadership*. Frank E Bird Jr and George L Germain. Institute Publishing 1986. ISBN 0 88061 054 9.

APPENDIX 1

The ways of securing the health and safety of people at work and protection of the public affected by work activities are established in Great Britain by law. In 1974 the Health and Safety at Work Act (HSW Act) set out the relevant responsibilities of employers and of people at work.

The HSW Act put duties on employers, the self-employed, employees, controllers of premises, designers, manufacturers, importers and suppliers. It requires that, so far as is reasonably practicable, premises, equipment, systems of work and articles for use at work are all safe and without risks to health. Supporting Acts and Regulations deal with particular hazards and types of work.

The Health and Safety Executive has a special responsibility to ensure that the HSW Act and other law on health and safety is observed. Its main instruments for this purpose are the Inspectorates listed below.

Through a network of 20 Area Offices throughout Great Britain, HSE inspectors review a wide range of work activities. They work mainly by giving expert advice and guidance, but they will, where necessary, issue enforcement notices and institute prosecutions.

HM FACTORY INSPECTORATE: manufacturing and heavy industrial premises and processes, as well as construction activities, local authority undertakings, hospitals, schools, universities and fairgrounds.

HM AGRICULTURE INSPECTORATE: farms, horticulture and forestry.

HM EXPLOSIVES INSPECTORATE: the manufacture, transport, handling and security of explosives.

HM MINES AND QUARRIES INSPECTORATE: all mines and quarries.

HM NUCLEAR INSTALLATIONS INSPECTORATE: which on HSE's behalf licenses nuclear installations ranging from nuclear power stations and nuclear chemical works to research reactors.

LOCAL AUTHORITIES: In most commercial undertakings enforcement of the legislation is undertaken by officers of the Local Authority.

All this work depends on close co-operation between field inspectors, policy branches, specialist inspectors, technical and scientific staff involved in research, testing, sampling and measuring activities and the Employment Medical Advisory Service.

Information about HSE and its work can be obtained from enquiry points at:

Baynards House,
1 Chepstow Place,
Westbourne Grove,
London W2 4TF
(Tel: 071-221 0870 Ext 6721/6722)

Broad Lane,
Sheffield S3 7HQ
(Tel: 0742 72539 Ext 3113/3114)

St Hugh's House,
Stanley Precinct,
Bootle,
Merseyside L20 3QY
(Tel: 051-951 4381)
Prestel: HSE lead frame No '575'.